THE BEAUTY QUEEN OF LEENANE

BY MARTIN McDONAGH

★

★

DRAMATISTS
PLAY SERVICE
INC.

THE BEAUTY QUEEN OF LEENANE
Copyright © 1996, 1999, Martin McDonagh

All Rights Reserved

SPECIAL NOTE

SPECIAL NOTE ON SONGS AND RECORDINGS

THE BEAUTY QUEEN OF LEENANE, was produced by Druid Theatre Company/Royal Court Theatre, at Town Hall Theatre, Galway, Ireland, on February 1, 1996. The production subsequently opened at the Royal Court Theatre Upstairs in London, England, on March 5, 1996. It was directed by Garry Hynes; the set design was by Francis O'Connor; the lighting design was by Ben Ormerod; the sound design was by David Murphy; original music was by Paddy Cunneen; and the production managers were Maurice Power (Druid) and Ed Wilson (RCT). The cast was as follows:

MAG FOLAN . . . . Anna Manahan
MAUREEN FOLAN . . . . Marie Mullen
RAY DOOLEY . . . . Tom Murphy
PATO DOOLEY . . . . Brían F. O'Byrne

The production was subsequently produced by Atlantic Theater Company, in New York City, on February 11, 1998. It then opened on Broadway, produced by Atlantic Theater Company, Randall L. Wreghitt, Chase Mishkin, Steven M. Levy and Leonard Soloway in association with Julian Schlossberg and Norma Langworthy, on April 14, 1998.

CHARACTERS

MAUREEN FOLAN — aged forty. Plain, slim.

MAG FOLAN — her mother, aged seventy. Stout, frail.

PATO DOOLEY — a good-looking local man, aged about forty.

RAY DOOLEY — his brother, aged twenty.

SETTING

Leenane, a small town in Connemara, County Galway.

THE BEAUTY QUEEN
OF LEENANE

ACT ONE

Scene 1

The living-room/kitchen of a rural cottage in the west of Ire-land. Front door stage left, a long black range along the back wall with a box of turf beside it and a rocking-chair on its right. On the kitchen side of the set is a door in the back wall leading off to an unseen hallway, and a newer oven, a sink and some cupboards curving around the right wall. There is a window with an inner ledge above the sink in the right wall looking out onto fields, a dinner table with two chairs just right of centre, a small TV down left, an electric kettle and a radio on one of the kitchen cupboards, a crucifix and a framed pic-ture of John and Robert Kennedy on the wall above the range, a heavy black poker beside the range, and a touristy-looking embroidered tea-towel hanging further along the back wall, bearing the inscription 'May you be half an hour in Heaven afore the Devil knows you're dead.' As the play begins it is raining quite heavily. Mag Folan, a stoutish woman in her early seventies with short, tightly permed grey hair and a mouth that gapes slightly, is sitting in the rocking-chair, staring off into space. Her left hand is somewhat more shrivelled and red than her right. The front door opens and her daughter, Mau-reen, a plain, slim woman of about forty, enters carrying shop-ping and goes through to the kitchen.

MAG.   Wet, Maureen?

MAUREEN.   Of course wet.

MAG.   Oh-h. *(Maureen takes her coat off, sighing, and starts putting the shopping away.)* I did take me Complan.

MAUREEN.   So you *can* get it yourself so.

MAG.   I can. *(Pause.)* Although lumpy it was, Maureen.

MAUREEN.   Well, can I help lumpy?

MAG.   No.

MAUREEN.   Write to the Complan people so, if it's lumpy.

MAG.   *(Pause.)* You do make me Complan nice and smooth. *(Pause.)* Not a lump at all, nor the comrade of a lump.

MAUREEN.   You don't give it a good enough stir is what you don't do.

MAG.   I gave it a good enough stir and there was still lumps.

MAUREEN.   You probably pour the water in too fast so. What it says on the box, you're supposed to ease it in.

MAG.   Mm.

MAUREEN.   That's where you do go wrong. Have another go tonight for yourself and you'll see.

MAG.   Mm. *(Pause.)* And the hot water too I do be scared of. Scared I may scould meself. *(Maureen gives her a slight look.)* I *do* be scared, Maureen. I be scared what if me hand shook and I was to pour it over me hand. And with you at Mary Pender's, then where would I be?

MAUREEN.   You're just a hypochondriac is what you are.

MAG.   I'd be lying on the floor and I'm not a hypochondriac.

MAUREEN.   You are too and everybody knows that you are. Full well.

MAG.   Don't I have a urine infection if I'm such a hypochondriac?

MAUREEN.   I can't see how a urine infection prevents you pouring a mug of Complan or tidying up the house a bit when I'm away. It wouldn't kill you.

MAG.   *(Pause.)* Me bad back.

MAUREEN.   Your back back.

MAG.   And me bad hand. *(Mag holds up her shrivelled hand for a second.)*

MAUREEN.   *(Quietly.)* Feck.... *(Irritated.)* I'll get your Complan so if it's such a big job! From now and 'til doomsday! The one thing I ask you to do. Do you see Annette or Margo coming pouring your Complan or buying your oul cod in butter sauce for the week?

MAG. No.

MAUREEN. No is right, you don't. And carrying it up that hill. And still I'm not appreciated.

MAG. You *are* appreciated, Maureen.

MAUREEN. I'm not appreciated.

MAG. I'll give me Complan another go so, and give it a good stir for meself.

MAUREEN. Ah, forget your Complan. I'm expected to do everything else, I suppose that one on top of it won't hurt. Just a ... just a blessed fecking skivvy is all I'm thought of!

MAG. You're not, Maureen. (*Maureen slams a couple of cupboard doors after finishing with the shopping and sits at the table, after dragging its chair back loudly. Pause.*) Me porridge, Maureen, I haven't had, will you be getting? No, in a minute, Maureen, have a rest for yourself.... (*But Maureen has already jumped up, stomped angrily back to the kitchen and started preparing the porridge as noisily as she can. Pause.*) Will we have the radio on for ourselves? (*Maureen bangs an angry finger at the radio's 'on' switch. It takes a couple of swipes before it comes on loudly, through static — a nasally male voice singing in Gaelic. Pause.*) The dedication Annette and Margo sent we still haven't heard. I wonder what's keeping it?

MAUREEN. If they sent a dedication at all. They only said they did. (*Maureen sniffs the sink a little, then turns to Mag.*) Is there a smell off this sink now, I'm wondering.

MAG. (*Defensively.*) No.

MAUREEN. I hope there's not, now.

MAG. No smell at all is there, Maureen. I do promise, now. (*Maureen returns to the porridge. Pause.*) Is the radio a biteen loud there, Maureen?

MAUREEN. A biteen loud, is it? (*Maureen swipes angrily at the radio again, turning it off. Pause.*)

MAG. Nothing on it, anyways. An oul fella singing nonsense.

MAUREEN. Isn't it you wanted it set for that oul station?

MAG. Only for Ceilidh Time and for whatyoucall.

7

MAUREEN. It's too late to go complaining now.

MAG. Not for nonsense did I want it set.

MAUREEN. *(Pause.)* It isn't nonsense anyways. Isn't it Irish?

MAG. It sounds like nonsense to me. Why can't they just speak English like everybody?

MAUREEN. Why should they speak English?

MAG. To know what they're saying.

MAUREEN. What country are you living in?

MAG. Eh?

MAUREEN. What country are you living in?

MAG. Galway.

MAUREEN. Not what county!

MAG. Oh-h....

MAUREEN. Ireland you're living in!

MAG. *Ireland.*

MAUREEN. So why should you be speaking English in Ireland?

MAG. I don't know why.

MAUREEN. It's Irish you should be speaking in Ireland.

MAG. It is.

MAUREEN. Eh?

MAG. Eh?

MAUREEN. 'Speaking English in Ireland.'

MAG. *(Pause.)* Except where would Irish get you going for a job in England? Nowhere.

MAUREEN. Well, isn't that the crux of the matter?

MAG. Is it, Maureen?

MAUREEN. If it wasn't for the English stealing our language, and our land, and our God-knows-what, wouldn't it be we wouldn't need to go over there begging for jobs and for handouts?

MAG. I suppose that's the crux of the matter.

MAUREEN. It *is* the crux of the matter.

MAG. *(Pause.)* Except America, too.

MAUREEN. What except America too?

MAG. If it was to America you had to go begging for handouts, it isn't Irish would be any good to you. It would be English!

MAUREEN. Isn't that the same crux of the same matter?

MAG. I don't know if it is or it isn't.

MAUREEN. Bringing up kids to think all they'll ever be good for is begging handouts from the English and the Yanks. That's the selfsame crux.

MAG. I suppose.

MAUREEN. Of course you suppose, because it's true.

MAG. *(Pause.)* If I had to go begging for handouts anywhere, I'd rather beg for them in America than in England, because in America it does be more sunny anyways. *(Pause.)* Or is that just something they say, that the weather is more sunny, Maureen? Or is that a lie, now? *(Maureen slops the porridge out and hands it to Mag, speaking as she does so.)*

MAUREEN. You're oul and you're stupid and you don't know what you're talking about. Now shut up and eat your oul porridge. *(Maureen goes back to wash the pan in the sink. Mag glances at the porridge, then turns back to her.)*

MAG. Me mug of tea you forgot! *(Maureen clutches the edges of the sink and lowers her head, exasperated, then quietly, with visible self-control, fills the kettle to make her mother's tea. Pause. Mag speaks while slowly eating.)* Did you meet anybody on your travels, Maureen? *(No response.)* Ah no, not on a day like today. *(Pause.)* Although you don't say hello to people is your trouble, Maureen. *(Pause.)* Although some people it would be better not to say hello to. The fella up and murdered the poor oul woman in Dublin and he didn't even know her. The news that story was on, did you hear of it? *(Pause.)* Strangled, and didn't even know her. That's a fella it would be better not to talk to. That's a fella it would be better to avoid outright. *(Maureen brings Mag her tea, then sits at the table.)*

MAUREEN. Sure, that sounds exactly the type of fella I would *like* to meet, and then bring him home to meet you, if he likes murdering oul women.

MAG. That's not a nice thing to say, Maureen.

MAUREEN. Is it not, now?

MAG. *(Pause.)* Sure why would he be coming all this way out from Dublin? He'd just be going out of his way.

MAUREEN. For the pleasure of me company he'd come.

Killing you, it'd just be a bonus for him.

MAG. Killing *you* I bet he first would be.

MAUREEN. I could live with that so long as I was sure he'd be clobbering you soon after. If he clobbered you with a big axe or something and took your oul head off and spat in your neck, I wouldn't mind at all, going first. Oh no, I'd enjoy it, I would. No more oul Complan to get, and no more oul porridge to get, and no more....

MAG. *(Interrupting, holding her tea out.)* No sugar in this, Maureen, you forgot, go and get me some. *(Maureen stares at her a moment, then takes the tea, brings it to the sink and pours it away, goes back to Mag, grabs her half-eaten porridge, returns to the kitchen, scrapes it out into the bin, leaves the bowl in the sink and exits into the hallway, giving Mag a dirty look on the way and closing the door behind her. Mag stares grumpily out into space. Blackout.)*

Scene 2

Mag is sitting at the table, staring at her reflection in a hand-mirror. She pats her hair a couple of times. The TV is on, showing an old episode of The Sullivans. *There is a knock at the front door, which startles her slightly.*

MAG. Who...? Maureen. Oh-h. The door, Maureen. *(Mag gets up and shuffles towards the kitchen window. There is another knock. She shuffles back to the door.)* Who's at the door?

RAY. *(Off.)* It's Ray Dooley, Mrs. From over the way.

MAG. Dooley?

RAY. Ray Dooley, aye. You know me.

MAG. Are you one of the Dooleys so?

RAY. I am. I'm Ray.

MAG. Oh-h.

RAY. *(Pause. Irritated.)* Well, will you let me in or am I going to talk to the door?

MAG. She's feeding the chickens. *(Pause.)* Have you gone?

RAY. *(Angrily.)* Open the oul door, Mrs.! Haven't I walked a mile out of me way just to get here?

MAG. Have you?

RAY. I have. 'Have you?' she says. *(Mag unlatches the door with some difficulty and Ray Dooley, a lad of about nineteen, enters.)* Thank you! An hour I thought you'd be keeping me waiting.

MAG. Oh, it's you, so it is.

RAY. Of course it's me. Who else?

MAG. You're the Dooley with the uncle.

RAY. It's only a million times you've seen me the past twenty year. Aye, I'm the Dooley with the uncle, and it's me uncle the message is. *(Ray stops and watches the TV a moment.)*

MAG. Maureen's at the chickens.

RAY. You've said Maureen's at the chickens. What's on the telly?

MAG. I was waiting for the news.

RAY. You'll have a long wait.

MAG. I was combing me hair.

RAY. I think it's *The Sullivans.*

MAG. I don't know what it is.

RAY. You do get a good reception.

MAG. A middling reception.

RAY. Everything's Australian nowadays.

MAG. I don't know if it is or it isn't. *(Mag sits in the rocking-chair.)* At the chickens, Maureen is.

RAY. That's three times now you've told me Maureen's at the chickens. Are you going for the world's record in saying 'Maureen's at the chickens'?

MAG. *(Pause. Confused.)* She's feeding them. *(Ray stares at her a moment, then sighs and looks out through the kitchen window.)*

RAY. Well, I'm not wading through all that skitter just to tell her. I've done enough wading. Coming up that oul hill.

MAG. It's a big oul hill.

RAY. It *is* a big oul hill.

MAG. Steep.

RAY. Steep is right and if not steep then muddy.

MAG. Muddy and rocky.

11

RAY. Muddy and rocky is right. Uh-huh. How do ye two manage up it every day?

MAG. We do drive.

RAY. Of course. *(Pause.)* That's what I want to do is drive. I'll have to be getting driving lessons. And a car. *(Pause.)* Not a good one, like. A second-hand one, y'know?

MAG. A used one.

RAY. A used one, aye.

MAG. Off somebody.

RAY. Oul Father Welsh — Walsh — has a car he's selling, but I'd look a poof buying a car off a priest.

MAG. I don't like Father Walsh — Welsh — at all.

RAY. He punched Mairtin Hanlon in the head once, and for no reason.

MAG. God love us!

RAY. Aye. Although, now, that was out of character for Father Welsh. Father Welsh seldom uses violence, same as most young priests. It's usually only the older priests go punching you in the head. I don't know why. I suppose it's the way they were brought up.

MAG. There was a priest the news Wednesday had a babby with a Yank!

RAY. That's no news at all. That's everyday. It'd be hard to find a priest who hasn't had a babby with a Yank. If he'd punched that babby in the head, that'd be news. Aye. Anyways. Aye. What was I saying? Oh aye, so if I give you the message, Mrs., you'll be passing it on to Maureen, so you will, or will I be writing it down for you?

MAG. I'll be passing it on.

RAY. Good-oh. Me brother Pato said to invite yous to our uncle's going-away do. The Riordan's hall out in Carraroe.

MAG. Is your brother back so?

RAY. He is.

MAG. Back from England?

RAY. Back from England, aye. England's where he was, so that's where he would be back from. Our Yankee uncle's going home to Boston after his holiday and taking those two ugly duckling daughters back with him and that Dolores whatyoucall,

12

Healey or Hooley, so there'll be a little to-do in the Riordan's as a good-bye or a *big* to-do knowing them show-off bastards and free food anyways, so me brother says ye're welcome to come or Maureen anyways, he knows you don't like getting out much. Isn't it you has the bad hip?

MAG. No.

RAY. Oh. Who is it has the bad hip so?

MAG. I don't know. I do have the urine infection.

RAY. Maybe that's what I was thinking of. And thanks for telling me.

MAG. Me urine.

RAY. I know, your urine.

MAG. And me bad back. And me burned hand.

RAY. Aye, aye, aye. Anyways, you'll be passing the message on to that one.

MAG. Eh?

RAY. You'll be remembering the message to pass it on to that one?

MAG. Aye.

RAY. Say it back to me so.

MAG. Say it back to you?

RAY. Aye.

MAG. *(Long pause.)* About me hip...?

RAY. *(Angrily.)* I should've fecking written it down in the first fecking place, I fecking knew! And save all this fecking time! *(Ray grabs a pen and a piece of paper, sits at the table and writes the message out.)* Talking with a loon!

MAG. *(Pause.)* Do me a mug of tea while you're here, Pato. Em, Ray.

RAY. *Ray* my fecking name is! Pato's me fecking brother!

MAG. I do forget.

RAY. It's like talking to a ... talking to a....

MAG. Brick wall.

RAY. Brick wall is right.

MAG. *(Pause.)* Or some soup do me. *(Ray finishes writing and gets up.)*

RAY. There. Forget about soup. The message is there. Point that one in the direction of it when she returns from beyond.

The Riordan's hall out in Carraroe. Seven o'clock tomorrow night. Free food. Okay?

MAG. All right now, Ray. Are you still in the choir nowadays, Ray?

RAY. I am *not* in the choir nowadays. Isn't it ten years since I was in the choir?

MAG. Doesn't time be flying?

RAY. Not since I took an interest in girls have I been in the choir because you do get no girls in choirs, only fat girls and what use are they? No. I go to discos, me.

MAG. Good enough for yourself.

RAY. What am I doing standing around here conversing with you? I have left me message and now I am off.

MAG. Good-bye to you, Ray.

RAY. Good-bye to you, Mrs.

MAG. And pull the door.

RAY. I was going to pull the door anyways.... (*Ray pulls the front door shut behind him as he exits. Off.*) I don't need your advice! (*As Ray's footsteps fade, Mag gets up, reads the message on the table, goes to the kitchen window and glances out, then finds a box of matches, comes back to the table, strikes a match, lights the message, goes to the range with it burning and drops it inside. Sound of footsteps approaching the front door. Mag shuffles back to her rocking chair and sits in it just as Maureen enters.*)

MAG. (*Nervously.*) Cold, Maureen?

MAUREEN. Of course cold.

MAG. Oh-h. (*Mag stares at the TV as if engrossed. Maureen sniffs the air a little, then sits at the table, staring at Mag.*)

MAUREEN. What are you watching?

MAG. I don't know *what* I'm watching. Just waiting for the news I am.

MAUREEN. Oh aye. (*Pause.*) Nobody rang while I was out, I suppose? Ah no.

MAG. Ah no, Maureen. Nobody did ring.

MAUREEN. Ah no.

MAG. No. Who would be ringing?

MAUREEN. No, nobody I suppose. No. (*Pause.*) And nobody

visited us either? Ah no.

MAG.   Ah no, Maureen. Who would be visiting us?

MAUREEN.   Nobody, I suppose. Ah no. *(Mag glances at Maureen a second, then back at the TV. Pause. Maureen gets up, ambles over to the TV, lazily switches it off with the toe of her shoe, ambles back to the kitchen, staring at Mag as she passes, turns on the kettle, and leans against the cupboards, looking back in Mag's direction.)*

MAG.   *(Nervously.)* Em, apart from wee Ray Dooley who passed.

MAUREEN.   *(Knowing.)* Oh, did Ray Dooley pass, now?

MAG.   He passed, aye, and said hello as he was passing.

MAUREEN.   I thought just now you said there was no visitors.

MAG.   There was no visitors, no, apart from Ray Dooley who passed.

MAUREEN.   Oh, aye, aye, aye. Just to say hello he popped his head in.

MAG.   Just to say hello and how is all. Aye. A nice wee lad he is.

MAUREEN.   Aye. *(Pause.)* With no news?

MAG.   With no news. Sure, what news would a gasur have?

MAUREEN.   None at all, I suppose. Ah, no.

MAG.   Ah no. *(Pause.)* Thinking of getting a car I think he said he was.

MAUREEN.   Oh aye?

MAG.   A second-hand one.

MAUREEN.   Uh-huh?

MAG.   To drive, y'know?

MAUREEN.   To drive, aye.

MAG.   Off Father Welsh — Walsh — Welsh.

MAUREEN.   Welsh.

MAG.   Welsh. *(Maureen switches off the kettle, pours a sachet of Complan into a mug and fills it up with water.)*

MAUREEN.   I'll do you some of your Complan.

MAG.   Have I not had me Complan already, Maureen? I have.

MAUREEN.   Sure, another one won't hurt.

MAG.   *(Wary.)* No, I suppose. *(Maureen tops the drink up with tap water to cool it, stirs it just twice to keep it lumpy, takes the spoon out, hands the drink to Mag, then leans back against the table to watch her drink it. Mag looks at it in distaste.)* A bit lumpy, Maureen.

MAUREEN. Never mind lumpy, mam. The lumps will do you good. That's the best part of Complan is the lumps. Drink ahead.

MAG. A little spoon, do you have?

MAUREEN. No, I have no little spoon. There's no little spoons for liars in this house. No little spoons at all. Be drinking ahead. *(Mag takes the smallest of sickly sips.)* The whole of it, now!

MAG. I do have a funny tummy, Maureen, and I do have no room.

MAUREEN. Drink ahead, I said! You had room enough to be spouting your lies about Ray Dooley had no message! Did I not meet him on the road beyond as he was going? The lies of you. The whole of that Complan you'll drink now, and suck the lumps down too, and whatever's left you haven't drank, it is over your head I will be emptying it, and you know well enough I mean it! *(Mag slowly drinks the rest of the sickly brew.)* Arsing me around, eh? interfering with my life again? Isn't it enough I've had to be on beck and call for you every day for the past twenty year? Is it one evening out you begrudge me?

MAG. Young girls should not be out gallivanting with fellas...!

MAUREEN. Young girls! I'm forty years old, for feck's sake! Finish it! *(Mag drinks again.)* 'Young girls'! That's the best yet. And how did Annette or Margo ever get married if it wasn't first out gallivanting that they were?

MAG. I don't know.

MAUREEN. Drink!

MAG. I don't like it, Maureen.

MAUREEN. Would you like it better over your head? *(Mag drinks again.)* I'll tell you, eh? 'Young girls out gallivanting.' I've heard it all now. What have I ever done but *kissed* two men the past forty year?

MAG. Two men is plenty!

MAUREEN. Finish!

MAG. I've finished! *(Mag holds out the mug. Maureen washes it.)* Two men is two men too much!

MAUREEN. To you, maybe. To you. Not to me.

MAG. Two men too much!

MAUREEN. Do you think I like being stuck up here with you?

Eh? Like a dried up oul....

MAG. Whore! *(Maureen laughs.)*

MAUREEN. 'Whore'? *(Pause.)* Do I not *wish*, now? Do I not wish? *(Pause.)* Sometimes I *dream*....

MAG. Of being a...?

MAUREEN. Of anything! *(Pause. Quietly.)* Of anything. Other than this.

MAG. Well an odd dream that is!

MAUREEN. It's not at all. Not at all is it an odd dream. *(Pause.)* And if it is it's not the only odd dream I do have. Do you want to be hearing another one?

MAG. I don't.

MAUREEN. I have a dream sometimes there of you, dressed all nice and white, in your coffin there, and me all in black looking in on you, and a fella beside me there, comforting me, the smell of aftershave off him, his arm round me waist. And the fella asks me then if I'll be going for a drink with him at his place after.

MAG. And what do you say?

MAUREEN. I say 'Aye, what's stopping me now?'

MAG. You don't!

MAUREEN. I do!

MAG. At me funeral?

MAUREEN. At your bloody wake, sure! Is even sooner!

MAG. Well that's not a nice thing to be dreaming!

MAUREEN. I know it's not, sure, and it isn't a *dream*-dream at all. It's more of a day-dream. Y'know, something happy to be thinking of when I'm scraping the skitter out of them hens.

MAG. Not at all is that a nice dream. That's a mean dream.

MAUREEN. I don't know if it is or it isn't. *(Pause. Maureen sits at the table with a pack of Kimberley biscuits.)* I suppose now you'll never be dying. You'll be hanging on forever, just to spite me.

MAG. I *will* be hanging on forever!

MAUREEN. I know well you will!

MAG. Seventy you'll be at my wake, and then how many men'll there be round your waist with their aftershave?

MAUREEN. None at all, I suppose.

MAG. None at all is right!

MAUREEN. Oh aye. *(Pause.)* Do you want a Kimberley?

MAG. *(Pause.)* Have we no shortbread fingers?

MAUREEN. No, you've ate all the shortbread fingers. Like a pig.

MAG. I'll have a Kimberley so, although I don't like Kimberleys. I don't know why you get Kimberleys at all. Kimberleys are horrible.

MAUREEN. Me world doesn't revolve around your taste in biscuits. *(Maureen gives Mag a biscuit. Mag eats.)*

MAG. *(Pause.)* You'll be going to this do tomorrow so?

MAUREEN. I will. *(Pause.)* It'll be good to see Pato again anyways. I didn't even know he was home.

MAG. But it's all them oul Yank'll be there tomorrow.

MAUREEN. So?

MAG. You said you couldn't stand the Yanks yesterday. The crux of the matter yesterday you said it was.

MAUREEN. Well, I suppose now, mother, I will have to be changing me mind, but, sure, isn't that a woman's prerogative?

MAG. *(Quietly.)* It's only prerogatives when it suits you.

MAUREEN. Don't go using big words you don't understand, now, mam.

MAG. *(Sneers. Pause.)* This invitation was open to me too, if you'd like to know.

MAUREEN. *(Half-laughing.)* Do you think you'll be coming?

MAG. I won't, I suppose.

MAUREEN. You suppose right enough. Lying the head off you, like the babby of a tinker.

MAG. I was only saying.

MAUREEN. Well, don't be saying. *(Pause.)* I think we might take a drive into Westport later, if it doesn't rain.

MAG. *(Brighter.)* Will we take a drive?

MAUREEN. We could take a little drive for ourselves.

MAG. We could now. It's a while since we did take a nice drive. We could get some shortbread fingers.

MAUREEN. Later on, I'm saying.

MAG. Later on. Not just now.

MAUREEN. Not just now. Sure, you've only just had your Complan now. *(Mag gives her a dirty look. Pause.)* Aye, Westport.

18

Aye. And I think I might pick up a nice little dress for meself while I'm there. For the do tomorrow, y'know? *(Maureen looks across at Mag, who looks back at her, irritated. Blackout.)*

Scene 3

Night. Set only just illuminated by the orange coals through the bars of the range. Radio has been left on low in the kitchen. Footsteps and voices of Maureen and Pato are heard outside, both slightly drunk.

PATO. *(Off, singing.)* 'The Cadillac stood by the house....'

MAUREEN. *(Off.)* Shh, Pato....

PATO. *(Off. Singing quietly.)* 'And the Yanks they were within.' *(Speaking.)* What was it that oul fella used to say, now?

MAUREEN. *(Off.)* What oul fella, now? *(Maureen opens the door and the two of them enter, turning the lights on. Maureen is in a new black dress, cut quite short. Pato Dooley is a good-looking man of about the same age as her.)*

PATO. The oul fella who used to chase oul whatyoucall. Oul Bugs Bunny.

MAUREEN. Would you like a cup of tea, Pato?

PATO. I would. *(Maureen switches the kettle on.)*

MAUREEN. Except keep your voice down, now.

PATO. *(Quietly.)* I will, I will. *(Pause.)* I can't remember *what* he used to say. The oul fella used to chase Bugs Bunny. It was something, now.

MAUREEN. Look at this. The radio left on too, the daft oul bitch.

PATO. Sure, what harm? No, leave it on, now. It'll cover up the sounds.

MAUREEN. What sounds?

PATO. The smooching sounds. *(He gently pulls her to him and they kiss a long while, then stop and look at each other. The kettle has*

19

boiled. Maureen gently breaks away, smiling, and starts making the tea.)
MAUREEN. Will you have a biscuit with your tea?
PATO. I will. What biscuits do you have, now?
MAUREEN. Em, only Kimberleys.
PATO. I'll leave it so, Maureen. I do hate Kimberleys. In fact I think Kimberleys are the most horrible biscuits in the world.
MAUREEN. The same as that, I hate Kimberleys. I only get them to torment me mother.
PATO. I can't see why the Kimberley people go making them at all. Coleman Connor ate a whole pack of Kimberleys one time and he was sick for a week. *(Pause.)* Or was it Mikados? It was some kind of horrible biscuits.
MAUREEN. Is it true Coleman cut the ears off Valene's dog and keeps them in his room in a bag?
PATO. He showed me them ears one day.
MAUREEN. That's awful spiteful, cutting the ears off a dog.
PATO. It *is* awful spiteful.
MAUREEN. It would be spiteful enough to cut the ears off anybody's dog, let alone your own brother's dog.
PATO. And it had seemed a nice dog.
MAUREEN. Aye. *(Pause.)* Aye. *(Awkward pause. Pato cuddles up behind her.)*
PATO. You feel nice to be giving a squeeze to.
MAUREEN. Do I?
PATO. Very nice. *(Maureen continues making the tea as Pato holds her. A little embarrassed and awkward, he breaks away from her after a second and idles a few feet away.)*
MAUREEN. Be sitting down for yourself, now, Pato.
PATO. I will. *(Sits at table.)* I do do what I'm told, I do.
MAUREEN. Oh-ho, do you now? That's the first time tonight I did notice. Them stray oul hands of yours.
PATO. Sure, I have no control over me hands. They have a mind of their own. *(Pause.)* Except I didn't notice you complaining overmuch anyways, me stray oul hands. Not too many complaints at all!
MAUREEN. I had complaints when they were straying over that Yank girl earlier on in the evening.
PATO. Well, I hadn't noticed you there at that time, Maureen.

How was I to know the beauty queen of Leenane was still yet to arrive?

MAUREEN. 'The beauty queen of Leenane.' Get away with ya!

PATO. Is true!

MAUREEN. Why so have no more than two words passed between us the past twenty year?

PATO. Sure, it's took me all this time to get up the courage.

MAUREEN. *(Smiling.)* Ah, bollocks to ya! *(Pato smiles. Maureen brings the tea over and sits down.)*

PATO. I don't know, Maureen. I don't know.

MAUREEN. Don't know what?

PATO. Why I never got around to really speaking to you or asking you out or the like. I don't know. Of course, hopping across to that bastarding oul place every couple of months couldn't've helped.

MAUREEN. England? Aye. Do you not like it there so?

PATO. *(Pause.)* It's money. *(Pause.)* And it's Tuesday I'll be back there again.

MAUREEN. Tuesday? This Tuesday?

PATO. Aye. *(Pause.)* It was only to see the Yanks off I was over. To say hello and say good-bye. No time back at all.

MAUREEN. That's Ireland, anyways. There's always someone leaving.

PATO. It's always the way.

MAUREEN. Bad, too.

PATO. What can you do?

MAUREEN. Stay?

PATO. *(Pause.)* I do ask meself, if there was good work in Leenane, would I stay in Leenane? I mean, there never will be good work, but hypothetically, I'm saying. Or even bad work. Any work. And when I'm over there in London and working in rain and it's more or less cattle I am, and the young fellas cursing over cards and drunk and sick, and the oul digs over there, all pee-stained mattresses and nothing to do but watch the clock ... when it's there I am, it's here I wish I was, of course. Who wouldn't? But when it's here I am ... it isn't *there* I want to be, of course not. But I know it isn't here I want to be either.

MAUREEN. And why, Pato?

PATO. I can't put my finger on why. *(Pause.)* Of course it's beautiful here, a fool can see. The mountains and the green, and people speak. But when everybody knows everybody else's business ... I don't know. *(Pause.)* You can't kick a cow in Leenane without some bastard holding a grudge twenty year.

MAUREEN. It's true enough.

PATO. It is. In England they don't care if you live or die, and it's funny but that isn't altogether a bad thing. Ah, sometimes it is ... ah, I don't know.

MAUREEN. *(Pause.)* Do you think you'll ever settle down in the one place so, Pato? When you get married, I suppose.

PATO. *(Half-laughing.)* 'When I get married....'

MAUREEN. You will someday, I'll bet you, get married. Wouldn't you want to?

PATO. I can't say it's something I do worry me head over.

MAUREEN. Of course, the rake of women you have stashed all over, you wouldn't need to.

PATO. *(Smiling.)* I have no rake of women.

MAUREEN. You have one or two, I bet.

PATO. I may have one or two. That I know to say hello to, now.

MAUREEN. Hello me.... A-hole.

PATO. Is true. *(Pause.)* Sure, I'm no....

MAUREEN. *(Pause.)* No what? *(Pause. Pato shrugs and shakes his head, somewhat sadly. Pause. The song "The Spinning Wheel,"* sung by Delia Murphy, has just started on the radio. Maureen continues.)* Me mother does love this oul song. Oul Delia Murphy.

PATO. This is a creepy oul song.

MAUREEN. It *is* a creepy oul song.

PATO. She does have a creepy oul voice. Always scared me this song did when I was a lad. She's like a ghoul singing. *(Pause.)* Does the grandmother die at the end, now, or is she just sleeping?

MAUREEN. Just sleeping, I think she is.

PATO. Aye....

MAUREEN. *(Pause.)* While the two go hand in hand through the fields.

PATO. Aye.

---

*See Special Note on Songs and Recordings on copyright page.

MAUREEN. Be moonlight.

PATO. *(Nods.)* They don't write songs like that any more. Thank Christ. *(Maureen laughs. Brighter.)* Wasn't it a grand night though, Maureen, now?

MAUREEN. It was.

PATO. Didn't we send them on their way well?

MAUREEN. We did, we did.

PATO. Not a dry eye.

MAUREEN. Indeed.

PATO. Eh?

MAUREEN. Indeed.

PATO. Aye. That we did. That we did.

MAUREEN. *(Pause.)* So who *was* the Yankee girl you did have your hands all over?

PATO. *(Laughing.)* Oh, will you stop it with your 'hands all over'?! Barely touched her, I did.

MAUREEN. Oh-ho!

PATO. A second cousin of me uncle, I think she is. Dolores somebody. Healey or Hooley. Healey. Boston, too, she lives.

MAUREEN. That was illegal so if it's your second cousin she is.

PATO. Illegal me arse, and it's not *my* second cousin she is anyway, and what's so illegal? Your second cousin's boobs aren't out of bounds, are they?

MAUREEN. They are!

PATO. I don't know about that. I'll have to consult with me lawyer on that one. I may get arrested the next time. And I have a defence anyways. She had dropped some Taytos on her blouse, there, I was just brushing them off for her.

MAUREEN. Taytos me arsehole, Pato Dooley!

PATO. Is true! *(Lustful pause. Nervously.)* Like this is all it was.... *(Pato slowly reaches out and gently brushes at, then gradually fondles, Maureen's breasts. She caresses his hand as he's doing so, then slowly gets up and sits across his lap, fondling his head as he continues touching her.)*

MAUREEN. She was prettier than me.

PATO. You're pretty.

MAUREEN. She was prettier.

PATO. I like you.

MAUREEN. You have blue eyes.

PATO. I do.

MAUREEN. Stay with me tonight.

PATO. I don't know, now, Maureen.

MAUREEN. Stay. Just tonight.

PATO. *(Pause.)* Is your mother asleep?

MAUREEN. I don't care if she is or she isn't. *(Pause.)* Go lower. *(Pato begins easing his hands down her front.)* Go lower.... Lower.... *(His hands reach her crotch. She tilts her head back slightly. The song on the radio ends. Blackout.)*

Scene 4

Morning. Maureen's black dress is lying across the table. Mag enters from the hall carrying a potty of urine, which she pours out down the sink. She exits into the hall to put the potty away and returns a moment later, wiping her empty hands on the sides of her nightie. She spots the black dress and picks it up disdainfully.

MAG. Forty pounds just for that skimpy dress? That dress is just skimpy. And laying it around then? *(She tosses the dress into a far corner, returns to the kitchen and switches the kettle on, speaking loudly to wake Maureen.)* I suppose I'll have to be getting me own Complan too, the hour you dragged yourself in whatever time it was with your oul dress. *(Quietly.)* That dress just looks silly. *(Loudly.)* Go the whole hog and wear no dress would be nearer the mark! *(Quietly.)* Snoring the head off you all night. Making an oul woman get her Complan, not to mention her porridge. Well, I won't be getting me own porridge, I'll tell you that now. I'd be afeard. You won't catch me getting me own porridge. Oh no. You won't be catching me out so easily. *(Pato has just entered from the hall, dressed in trousers and pulling on a shirt.)*

24

PATO. Good morning there, now, Mrs. *(Mag is startled, staring at Pato dumbfounded.)*

MAG. Good morning there, now.

PATO. Is it porridge you're after?

MAG. It is.

PATO. I'll be getting your porridge for you, so, if you like.

MAG. Oh-h.

PATO. Go ahead and rest yourself. *(Mag sits in the rocking chair, keeping her eyes on Pato all the while as he prepares her porridge.)* It's many the time I did get me brother his porridge of a school morning, so I'm well accustomed. *(Pause.)* You couldn't make it to the oul Yanks' do yesterday so?

MAG. No.

PATO. Your bad hip it was, Maureen was saying.

MAG. *(Still shocked.)* Aye, me bad hip. *(Pause.)* Where's Maureen, now?

PATO. Em, having a lie-in a minute or two, she is. *(Pause.)* To tell you the truth, I was all for ... I was all for creeping out before ever you got yourself up, but Maureen said, 'Aren't we all adults, now? What harm?' I suppose we are, but ... I don't know. It's still awkward, now, or something. D'you know what I mean? I don't know. *(Pause.)* The Yanks'll be touching down in Boston about now anyways. God willing anyways. Aye. *(Pause.)* A good oul send-off we gave them anyways, we did, to send them off. Aye. *(Pause.)* Not a dry eye. *(Pause.)* Aye. *(Pause.)* Was it a mug of Complan too you wanted?

MAG. It was. *(Pato fixes her Complan and brings it over.)*

PATO. You like your Complan so.

MAG. I don't.

PATO. Do you not, now?

MAG. She makes me drink it when I don't like it and forces me.

PATO. But Complan's good for you anyways if you're old.

MAG. I suppose it's good for me.

PATO. It is. Isn't it chicken flavour?

MAG. I don't know what flavour.

PATO. *(Checking box.)* Aye, it's chicken flavour. That's the best flavour. *(Pato returns to the porridge.)*

MAG. *(Quietly.)* With all oul lumps you do make it, never minding flavour. *And* no spoon. *(Pato gives Mag her porridge and sits at the table.)*

PATO. There you go, now. *(Pause.)* Whatever happened to your hand there, Mrs.? Red raw, it is.

MAG. Me hand, is it?

PATO. Was it a scould you did get?

MAG. It *was* a scould.

PATO. You have to be careful with scoulds at your age.

MAG. Careful, is it? Uh-huh.... *(Maureen enters from the hall, wearing only a bra and slip, and goes over to Pato.)*

MAUREEN. Careful what? We was careful, weren't we, Pato? *(Maureen sits across Pato's lap.)*

PATO. *(Embarrassed.)* Maureen, now....

MAUREEN. Careful enough, cos we don't need any babies coming, do we? We do have enough babies in this house to be going on with. *(Maureen kisses him at length. Mag watches in disgust.)*

PATO. Maureen, now....

MAUREEN. Just thanking you for a wonderful night, I am, Pato. Well worth the wait it was. *Well* worth the wait.

PATO. *(Embarrassed.)* Good-oh.

MAG. Discussing me scoulded hand we was before you breezed in with no clothes!

MAUREEN. Ar, feck your scoulded hand. *(To Pato.)* You'll have to be putting that thing of yours in me again before too long is past, Pato. I do have a taste for it now, I do....

PATO. Maureen.... *(She kisses him, gets off, and stares at Mag as she passes into the kitchen.)*

MAUREEN. A mighty oul taste. Uh-huh. *(Pato gets up and idles around in embarrassment.)*

PATO. Em, I'll have to be off now in a minute anyways. I do have packing to do I do, and whatyoucall....

MAG. *(Pointing at Maureen. Loudly.)* She's the one that scoulded me hand! I'll tell you that, now! Let alone sitting on stray men! Held it down on the range she did! Poured chip-pan fat o'er it! Aye, and told the doctor it was me!

MAUREEN. *(Pause. Nonplussed, to Pato.)* Be having a mug of tea before you go, Pato, now.

PATO.   *(Pause.)* Maybe a quick one. *(Maureen pours out the tea. Mag looks back and forth between the two of them.)*

MAG.   Did you not hear what I said?

MAUREEN.   Do you think Pato listens to the smutterings of a senile oul hen?

MAG.   Senile, is it? *(She holds up her left hand.)* Don't I have the evidence?

MAUREEN.   Come over here a second, Pato. I want you to smell this sink for me.

MAG.   Sinks have nothing to do with it!

MAUREEN.   Come over here now, Pato.

PATO.   Eh? *(Pato goes into the kitchen.)*

MAUREEN.   Smell that sink. *(Pato leans into the sink, sniffs it, then pulls his head away in disgust.)*

MAG.   Nothing to do with it, sinks have!

MAUREEN.   Nothing to do with it, is it? Everything to do with it, *I* think it has. Serves as evidence to the character of me accuser, it does.

PATO.   What is that, now? The drains?

MAUREEN.   Not the drains at all. Not the drains at all. Doesn't she pour a potty of wee away down there every morning, though I tell her seven hundred times the lavvy to use, but oh no.

MAG.   Me scoulded hand this conversation was, and not wee at all?

MAUREEN.   And doesn't even rinse it either. Now is that hygienic? And she does have a urine infection too, is even less hygienic. I wash me praities in there. Here's your tea now, Pato. *(Pato takes his tea, sipping it squeamishly.)*

MAG.   Put some clothes on you, going around the house half-naked! Would be more in your line!

MAUREEN.   I do like going around the house half-naked. It does turn me on, it does.

MAG.   I suppose it does, aye.

MAUREEN.   It does.

MAG.   And reminds you of Difford Hall in England, too, I'll bet it does....

MAUREEN.   *(Angrily.)* Now you just shut your fecking....

MAG. None of your own clothes they let you wear in there either, did they?

MAUREEN. Shut your oul gob, I said...!

MAG. Only long oul gowns and buckle-down jackets.... *(Maureen approaches Mag, fists clenched. Pato catches her arm and steps between the two.)*

PATO. What's the matter with ye two at all, now...?

MAG. Difford Hall! Difford Hall! Difford Hall...!

MAUREEN. Difford Hall, uh-huh. And I suppose....

MAG. Difford Hall! Difford Hall...!

MAUREEN. And I suppose that potty of wee was just a figment of me imagination?

MAG. Forget wee! Forget wee! D'you want to know what Difford Hall is, fella?

MAUREEN. Shut up, now!

MAG. It's a nut-house! An oul nut-house in England I did have to sign her out of and promise to keep her in me care. Would you want to be seeing the papers now? *(Mag shuffles off to the hall.)* As proof, like. Or to prove am I just a senile oul hen, like, or *who's* the loopy one? Heh! Pegging wee in me face, oh aye.... *(Quiet pause. Maureen idles over to the table and sits. Pato pours his tea down the sink, rinses his mug and washes his hands.)*

MAUREEN. *(Quietly.)* It's true I was in a home there a while, now, after a bit of a breakdown I had. Years ago this is.

PATO. What harm a breakdown, sure? Lots of people do have breakdowns.

MAUREEN. A lot of doolally people, aye.

PATO. Not doolally people at all. A lot of well-educated people have breakdowns too. In fact, it you're well-educated it's even more likely. Poor Spike Milligan, isn't he forever having breakdowns? He hardly stops. I do have trouble with me nerves every now and then, too, I don't mind admitting. There's no shame at all in that. Only means you do think about things, and take them to heart.

MAUREEN. No shame in being put in a nut-house a month? Ah no.

PATO. No shame in thinking about things and worrying about things, I'm saying, and 'nut-house' is a silly word to be using, and you know that well enough, now, Maureen.

MAUREEN. I do. *(Pato goes over and sits across the table from her.)* In England I was, this happened. Cleaning work. When I was twenty-five. Me first time ever. Me only time over. Me sister had just got married, me other sister just about to. Over in Leeds I was, cleaning offices. Bogs. A whole group of us, only them were all English. 'Ya oul backward Paddy fecking.... The fecking pig's-backside face on ya.' The first time out of Connemara this was I'd been. 'Get back to that backward fecking pigsty of yours or whatever hole it was you drug yourself out of.' Half of the swearing I didn't even understand. I had to have a black woman explain it to me. Trinidad she was from. They'd have a go at her too, but she'd just laugh. This big face she had, this big oul smile. And photos of Trinidad she'd show me, and 'What the hell have you left there for?' I'd say. 'To come to this place, cleaning shite?' And a calendar with a picture of Connemara on I showed her one day, and 'What the hell have you left there for?' she said back to me. 'To come to this place....' *(Pause.)* But she moved to London then, her husband was dying. And after that it all just got to me.

PATO. *(Pause.)* That's all past and behind you now anyways, Maureen. *(Pause. Maureen looks at him a while.)*

MAUREEN. Am I still a nut case you're saying, or you're wondering?

PATO. Not at all, now....

MAUREEN. Oh no...? *(Maureen gets up and wanders back to the kitchen.)*

PATO. Not at all. That's a long time in the past is all I'm saying. And nothing to be ashamed of. Put it behind you, you should.

MAUREEN. Put it behind me, aye, with that one hovering eyeing me every minute, like I'm some kind of ... some kind of.... *(Pause.)* And, no, I didn't scould her oul hand, no matter how doolally I ever was. Trying to cook chips on her own, she was. We'd argued, and I'd left her on her own an hour, and chips she up and decided she wanted. She must've tipped the pan over. God knows how, the eej. I just found her lying there. Only, because of Difford Hall, she thinks any accusation she throws at me I won't be any the wiser. I won't be able to tell the differ, what's true and what's not. Well, I *am* able to tell the differ. Well able, the smelly oul bitch.

PATO. You shouldn't let her get to you, Maureen.

MAUREEN. How can I help it, Pato? She's enough to drive anyone loopy, if they weren't loopy to begin with.

PATO. *(Smiling.)* She is at that, I suppose.

MAUREEN. *(Smiling.)* She is. It's surprised I am how sane I've turned out! *(They both smile. Pause.)*

PATO. I *will* have to be off in a minute now, Maureen.

MAUREEN. Okay, Pato. Did you finish your tea, now?

PATO. I didn't. The talk of your mother's wee, it did put me off it.

MAUREEN. It would. It would anybody. Don't I have to live with it? *(Sadly.)* Don't I have to live with it? *(Looking straight at him.)* I suppose I do, Now.

PATO. *(Pause.)* Be putting on some clothes there, Maureen. You'll freeze with no fire down. *(Pause. Maureen's mood has become sombre again. She looks down at herself.)*

MAUREEN. *(Quietly.)* 'Be putting on some clothes'? Is it ugly you think I am now, so, 'Be putting on some clothes....'

PATO. No, Maureen, the cold, I'm saying. You can't go walking about.... You'll freeze, sure.

MAUREEN. It wasn't ugly you thought I was last night, or maybe it was, now.

PATO. No, Maureen, now. What...?

MAUREEN. A beauty queen you thought I was last night, or you said I was. When it's 'Cover yourself', now, 'You do sicken me'....

PATO. *(Approaching her.)* Maureen, no, now, what are you saying that for...?

MAUREEN. Maybe that was the reason so.

PATO. *(Stops.)* The reason what?

MAUREEN. Be off with you so, if I sicken you.

PATO. You don't sicken me.

MAUREEN. *(Almost crying.)* Be off with you, I said.

PATO. *(Approaching again.)* Maureen.... *(Mag enters, waving papers, stopping Pato's approach.)*

MAG. Eh? Here's the papers now, Difford Hall, if I'm such a

senile oul hen. Eh? Who wants an oul read, now? Eh? Proof this is, let alone pegging sinks at me! *(Pause.)* Eh?

PATO.   Maureen....

MAUREEN.   *(Composed. Gently.)* Be going now, Pato.

PATO.   *(Pause.)* I'll write to you from England. *(Pause. Sternly.)* Look at me! *(Pause. Softly.)* I'll write to you from England. *(Pato puts on his jacket, turns for a last look at Maureen, then exits, closing the door behind him. Footsteps away. Pause.)*

MAG.   He won't write at all. *(Pause.)* And I did throw your oul dress in that dirty corner too! *(Pause. Maureen looks at her a moment, sad, despairing but not angry.)*

MAUREEN.   Why? Why? Why do you...? *(Pause. Maureen goes over to where her dress is lying, crouches down beside it and picks it up, holding it to her chest. She lingers there a moment, then gets up and passes her mother.)* Just look at yourself. *(Maureen exits into hall.)*

MAG.   Just look at yourself too, would be ... would be ... *(Maureen shuts the hall door behind her.)* ... more in your line. *(Mag is still holding up the papers rather dumbly. Pause. She lays the papers down, scratches herself, notices her uneaten porridge and sticks a finger in it. Quietly.)* Me porridge is gone cold now. *(Loudly.)* Me porridge is gone cold now! *(Mag stares out front, blankly. Blackout. Interval.)*

ACT TWO

Scene 1

Most of the stage is in darkness apart from a spotlight or some such on Pato sitting at the table as if in a bedsit in England, reciting a letter he has written to Maureen.

PATO.   Dear Maureen, it is Pato Dooley and I'm writing from London, and I'm sorry it's taken so long to write to you but to be honest I didn't know whether you wanted me to one way or the other, so I have taken it upon myself to try and see. There are a lot of things I want to say but I am no letter-writer but I will try to say them if I can. Well, Maureen, there is no major news here, except a Wexford man on the site a day ago, a rake of bricks fell on him from the scaffold and forty stitches he did have in his head and was lucky to be alive at all, he was an old fella, or fifty-odd anyways, but apart from that there is no major news. I do go out for a pint of a Saturday or a Friday but I don't know nobody and don't speak to anyone. There is no one to speak to. The gangerman does pop his head in sometimes. I don't know if I've spelt it right, 'Gangerman', is it 'e-r' or is it 'a'? It is not a word we was taught in school. Well, Maureen, I am 'beating around the bush' as they say, because it is you and me I do want to be talking about, if there is such a thing now as 'you and me', I don't know the state of play. What I thought I thought we were getting on royally, at the good-bye to the Yanks and the part after when we did talk and went to yours. And I *did* think you were a beauty queen and I *do* think, and it wasn't anything to do with that at all or with you at all, I think you thought it was. All it was, it has happened to me a couple of times before when I've had a drink taken and was nothing to do with did I want to. I would have been honoured to be the first one you chose, and flattered, and the thing that I'm saying, I was honoured then and I am still honoured, and just because it was not

32

to be that night, does it mean it is not to be ever? I don't see why it should, and I don't see why you was so angry when you was so nice to me when it happened. I think you thought I looked at you differently when your breakdown business came up, when I didn't look at you differently at all, or the thing I said 'Put on your clothes, it's cold', when you seemed to think I did not want to be looking at you in your bra and slip there, when nothing could be further from the truth, because if truth be told I could have looked at you in your bra and slip until the cows came home. I could never get my fill of looking at you in your bra and slip, and some day, God-willing, I will be looking at you in your bra and slip again. Which leads me on to my other thing, unless you still haven't forgiven me, in which case we should just forget about it and part as friends, but if you *have* forgiven me it leads me on to my other thing which I was lying to you before when I said I had no news because I do have news. What the news is I have been in touch with me uncle in Boston and the incident with the Wexford man with the bricks was just the final straw. You'd be lucky to get away with your life the building sites in England, let alone the bad money and the 'You oul Irish this-and-that', and I have been in touch with me uncle in Boston and a job he has offered me there, and I am going to take him up on it. Back in Leenane two weeks tomorrow I'll be, to collect up my stuff and I suppose a bit of a do they'll throw me, and the thing I want to say to you is do you want to come with me? Not straight away of course, I know, because you would have things to clear up, but after a month or two I'm saying, but maybe you haven't forgiven me at all and it's being a fool I'm being. Well, if you haven't forgiven me I suppose it'd be best if we just kept out of each other's way the few days I'm over and if I don't hear from you I will understand, but if you *have* forgiven me what's to keep you in Ireland? There's your sisters could take care of your mother and why should you have had the burden all these years, don't you deserve a life? And if they say no, isn't there the home in Oughterard isn't ideal but they do take good care of them, my mother before she passed, and don't they have bingo and what good to your mother does that big hill do? No good. *(Pause.)* Anyways, Maureen, I will leave it up to you. My address is up the top there and the number of the phone in the hall, only let it ring a good while if you want to ring and you'll need the codes, and it would be grand to hear from you. If I don't hear from you, I will understand. Take good care of yourself, Maureen. And that night we shared, even if nothing happened, it still makes me happy just to think about it, being close to you, and even if I never hear from you again I'll always have a happy memory of that night, and that's all I wanted to say to you. Do think about it. Yours sincerely, Pato Dooley. *(Spotlight cuts out, but while the stage is in darkness Pato continues with a letter to his brother.)*

Dear Raymond, how are you? I'm enclosing a bunch of letters I don't want different people snooping in on. Will you hand them out for me and don't be reading them, I know you won't be. The one to Mick Dowd you can wait till he comes out of hospital. Let me know how he is or have they arrested the lass who belted him. The one to poor Girleen you can give to her any time you see her, it is only to tell her to stop falling in love with priests. But the one to Maureen Folan I want you to go over there the day you get this and put it in her hand. This is important now, in her hand put it. Not much other news here. I'll fill you in on more of the America details nearer the time. Yes, it's a great thing. Good luck to you, Raymond, and P.S. Remember now, in Maureen's hand put it. Good-bye.

Scene 2

Afternoon. Ray is standing near the lit range, watching TV, somewhat engrossed, tapping a sealed envelope against his knee now and then. Mag watches him and the letter from the rocking-chair. Long pause before Ray speaks.

RAY. That Wayne's an oul bastard.
MAG. Is he?
RAY. He is. He never stops.

MAG. Oh-h.

RAY. *(Pause.)* D'you see Patricia with the hair? Patricia's bad enough, but Wayne's a pure terror. *(Pause.)* I do like *Sons and Daughters*, I do.

MAG. Do ya?

RAY. Everybody's always killing each other and a lot of the girls do have swimsuits. That's the best kind of programme.

MAG. I'm just waiting for the news to come on.

RAY. *(Pause.)* You'll have a long wait. *(The programme ends. Ray stretches himself.)* That's that then.

MAG. Is the news not next? Ah no.

RAY. No. For God's sake, *A Country Fecking Practice*'s on next. Isn't it Thursday?

MAG. Turn it off, so, if the news isn't on. That's all I do be waiting for. *(Ray turns the TV off and idles around.)*

RAY. Six o'clock the news isn't on 'til. *(He glances at his watch. Quietly, irritated.)* Feck, feck, feck, feck, feck, feck, feck, feck, feck. *(Pause.)* You said she'd be home be now, didn't you?

MAG. I did. *(Pause.)* Maybe she got talking to somebody, although she doesn't usually get talking to somebody. She does keep herself to herself.

RAY. I know well she does keep herself to herself. *(Pause.)* Loopy that woman is, if you ask me. Didn't she keep the tennis ball that came off me and Mairtin Hanlon's swingball set and landed in yere fields and wouldn't give it back no matter how much we begged and that was ten years ago and I still haven't forgotten it?

MAG. I do have no comment, as they say.

RAY. Still haven't forgotten it and I never will forget it!

MAG. But wasn't it that you and Mairtin were pegging yere tennis ball at our chickens and clobbered one of them dead is why your ball was in our fields...?

RAY. It was swingball we were playing, Mrs.!

MAG. Oh-h.

RAY. Not clobbering at all. Swingball it was. And never again able to play swingball were we. For the rest of our youth, now. For what use is a swingball set without a ball?

MAG. No use.

35

RAY. No use is right! No use at all. *(Pause.) Bitch!*

MAG. *(Pause.)* Be off and give your letter to me so, Ray, now, and I'll make sure she gets it, and not have you waiting for a lass ruined your swingball set on you. *(Ray thinks about it, tempted, but grudgingly decides against it.)*

RAY. I'm under strict instructions now, Mrs.

MAG. *(Tuts.)* Make me a mug of tea so.

RAY. I'm not making you a mug of tea. Under duress is all I'm here. I'm not skivvying about on top of it.

MAG. *(Pause.)* Or another bit of turf on the fire put. I'm cold.

RAY. Did I not just say?

MAG. Ah g'wan, Ray. You're a good boy, God bless you. *(Sighing, Ray puts the letter — which Mag stares at throughout — on the table and uses the heavy black poker beside the range to pick some turf up and place it inside, stoking it afterwards.)*

RAY. Neverminding swingball, I saw her there on the road the other week and I said hello to her and what did she do? She outright ignored me. Didn't even look up.

MAG. Didn't she?

RAY. And what I thought of saying, I thought of saying, 'Up your oul hole, Mrs.', but I didn't say it, I just thought of saying it, but thinking back on it I should've gone ahead and said it and skitter on the bitch!

MAG. It would've been good enough for her to say it, up and ignoring you on the road, because you're a good gasur, Ray, fixing me fire for me. Ah, she's been in a foul oul mood lately.

RAY. She does wear horrible clothes. And everyone agrees. *(Finished at the range, poker still in hand, Ray looks over the tea-towel on the back wall.)* 'May you be half an hour in Heaven afore the Devil knows you're dead.'

MAG. Aye.

RAY. *(Funny voice.)* 'May you be half an hour in Heaven afore the Devil knows you're dead.'

MAG. *(Embarrassed laugh.)* Aye. *(Ray idles around a little, wielding the poker.)*

RAY. This is a great oul poker, this is.

MAG. Is it?

RAY. Good and heavy.

MAG. Heavy and long.

RAY. Good and heavy and long. A half a dozen coppers you could take out with this poker and barely notice and have not a scratch on it and then clobber them again just for the fun of seeing the blood running out of them. *(Pause.)* Will you sell it to me?

MAG. I will not. To go battering the polis?

RAY. A fiver.

MAG. We do need it for the fire, sure. *(Ray tuts and puts the poker back beside the range.)*

RAY. Sure, that poker's just going to waste in this house. *(Ray idles into the kitchen. Her eye on the letter, Mag slowly gets out of her chair.)* Ah, I could get a dozen pokers in town just as good if I wanted, and at half the price. *(Just as Mag starts her approach to the letter, Ray returns, not noticing her, idles past and picks the letter back up on his way. Mag grimaces slightly and sits back down. Ray opens the front door, glances out to see if Maureen is coming, then closes it again, sighing.)* A whole afternoon I'm wasting here. *(Pause.)* When I could be at home watching telly. *(Ray sits at the table.)*

MAG. You never know, it might be evening before she's ever home.

RAY. *(Angrily.)* You said three o'clock it was sure to be when I first came in!

MAG. Aye, three o'clock it usually is, oh aye. *(Pause.)* Just sometimes it does be evening. On occasion, like. *(Pause.)* Sometimes it does be *late* evening. *(Pause.)* Sometimes it does be *night.* *(Pause.)* *Morning* it was one time before she....

RAY. *(Interrupting angrily.)* All right, all right! It's thumping you in a minute I'll be!

MAG. *(Pause.)* I'm only saying now.

RAY. Well, stop saying! *(Sighs. Long pause.)* This house does smell of pee, this house does.

MAG. *(Pause. Embarrassed.)* Em, cats do get in.

RAY. Do cats get in?

MAG. They do. *(Pause.)* They do go to the sink.

RAY. *(Pause.)* What do they go to the sink for?

MAG. To wee.

RAY. To wee? They go to the sink to wee? *(Piss-taking.)* Sure,

37

that's mighty good of them. You do get a very considerate breed of cat up this way so.

MAG. *(Pause.)* I don't know what breed they are. *(Pause. Ray lets his head slump down onto the table with a bump, and slowly and rhythmically starts banging his fist down beside it.)*

RAY. *(Droning.)* I don't want to be here, I don't want to be here, I don't want to be here, I don't want to be here.... *(Ray lifts his head back up, stares at the letter, then starts slowly turning it around, end over end, sorely tempted.)*

MAG. *(Pause.)* Do me a mug of tea, Ray. *(Pause.)* Or a mug of Complan do me, even. *(Pause.)* And give it a good stir to get rid of the oul lumps.

RAY. If it was getting rid of oul lumps I was to be, it wouldn't be with Complan I'd be starting. It would be much closer to home, boy. Oh aye, much closer. A big lump sitting in an oul fecking rocking-chair it would be. I'll tell you that!

MAG. *(Pause.)* Or a Cup-a-Soup do me. *(Ray grits his teeth and begins breathing in and out through them, almost crying.)*

RAY. *(Giving in sadly.)* Pato, Pato, Pato. *(Pause.)* Ah what news could it be? *(Pause. Sternly.)* Were I to leave this letter here with you, Mrs., it would be straight to that one you would be giving it, isn't that right?

MAG. It is. Oh, straight to Maureen I'd be giving it.

RAY. *(Pause.)* And it isn't opening it you would be?

MAG. It is not. Sure, a letter is a private thing. If it isn't my name on it, what business would it be of mine?

RAY. And may God strike you dead if you do open it?

MAG. And may God strike me dead if I do open it, only He'll have no need to strike me dead because I won't be opening it.

RAY. *(Pause.)* I'll leave it so. *(Ray stands, places the letter up against a salt-cellar, thinks about it again for a moment, looks Mag over a second, looks back at the letter again, thinks once more, then waves a hand in a gesture of tired resignation, deciding to leave it.)* I'll be seeing you then, Mrs.

MAG. Be seeing you, Pato. *Ray,* I mean. *(Ray grimaces at her and exits through the front door, but leaves it slightly ajar, as he is still waiting outside. Mag places her hands on the sides of the rocking-chair, about to drag herself up, then warily remembers she hasn't heard Ray's footsteps away. She lets her hands rest back in her lap and sits back serenely. Pause. The front door bursts open and Ray sticks his head around it to look at her. She smiles at him innocently.)*

RAY. Good-oh. *(Ray exits again, closing the door behind him fully this time. Mag listens to his footsteps fading away, then gets up, picks up the envelope and opens it, goes back to the range and lifts off the lid so that the flames are visible, and stands there reading the letter. She drops the first short page into the flames as she finishes it, then starts reading the second. Slow fade-out.)*

Scene 3

Night. Mag is in her rocking-chair, Maureen at the table, reading. The radio is on low, tuned to a request show. The reception is quite poor, wavering and crackling with static. Pause before Mag speaks.

MAG. A poor reception.
MAUREEN. Can I help it if it's a poor reception?
MAG. *(Pause.)* Crackly. *(Pause.)* We can hardly hear the tunes. *(Pause.)* We can hardly hear what are the dedications or from what part of the country.
MAUREEN. I can hear well enough.
MAG. Can ya?
MAUREEN. *(Pause.)* Maybe it's deaf it is you're going.
MAG. It's not deaf I'm going. Not nearly deaf.
MAUREEN. It's a home for deaf people I'll have to be putting you in soon. *(Pause.)* And it isn't cod in butter sauce you'll be getting in there. No. Not by a long chalk. Oul beans on toast or something is all you'll be getting in there. If you're lucky. And then if you don't eat it, they'll give you a good kick, or maybe a punch.
MAG. *(Pause.)* I'd die before I'd let meself be put in a home.
MAUREEN. Hopefully, aye.

MAG. *(Pause.)* That was a nice bit of cod in butter sauce, Maureen.

MAUREEN. I suppose it was.

MAG. Tasty.

MAUREEN. All I do is boil it in the bag and snip it with a scissor. I hardly need your compliments.

MAG. *(Pause.)* Mean to me is all you ever are nowadays.

MAUREEN. If I am or if I'm not. *(Pause.)* Didn't I buy you a packet of wine gums last week if I'm so mean?

MAG. *(Pause.)* All because of Pato Dooley you're mean, I suppose. *(Pause.)* Him not inviting you to his oul going-away do tonight.

MAUREEN. Pato Dooley has his own life to lead.

MAG. Only after one thing that man was.

MAUREEN. Maybe he was, now. Or maybe it was me who was only after one thing. We do have equality nowadays. Not like in your day.

MAG. There was nothing wrong in my day.

MAUREEN. Allowed to go on top of a man nowadays, we are. All we have to do is ask. And nice it is on top of a man, too.

MAG. Is it nice now, Maureen?

MAUREEN. *(Bemused that Mag isn't offended.)* It is.

MAG. It does sound nice. Ah, good enough for yourself, now. *(Maureen, still bemused, gets some shortbread fingers from the kitchen and eats a couple.)* And not worried about having been put in the family way, are you?

MAUREEN. I'm not. We was careful.

MAG. Was ye careful?

MAUREEN. Aye. We was nice and careful. We was *lovely* and careful, if you must know.

MAG. I'll bet ye was lovely and careful, aye. Oh aye. Lovely and careful, I'll bet ye were.

MAUREEN. *(Pause.)* You haven't been sniffing the pariffin lamps again?

MAG. *(Pause.)* It's always the paraffin lamp business you do throw at me.

MAUREEN. It's a funny oul mood you're in so.

MAG.   Is it a funny oul mood? No. Just a normal mood, now.

MAUREEN.   It's a funny one. *(Pause.)* Aye, a great oul time me and Pato did have. I can see now what all the fuss did be about, but ah, there has to be more to a man than just being good in bed. Things in common too you do have to have, y'know, like what books do you be reading, or what are your politics and the like, so I did have to tell him it was no-go, no matter how good in bed he was.

MAG.   When was this you did tell him?

MAUREEN.   A while ago it was I did tell him. Back....

MAG.   *(Interrupting.)* And I suppose he was upset at that.

MAUREEN.   He *was* upset at that but I assured him it was for the best and he did seem to accept it then.

MAG.   I'll bet he accepted it.

MAUREEN.   *(Pause.)* But that's why I thought it would be unfair of me to go over to his do and wish him good-bye. I thought it would be awkward for him.

MAG.   It would be awkward for him, aye, I suppose. Oh aye. *(Pause.)* So all it was was ye didn't have enough things in common was all that parted ye?

MAUREEN.   Is all it was. And parted on amicable terms, and with no grudges on either side. *(Pause.)* No. No grudges at all. I did get what I did want out of Pato Dooley that night, and that was good enough for him, and that was good enough for me.

MAG.   Oh aye, now. I'm sure. It was good enough for the both of ye. Oh aye. *(Mag smiles and nods.)*

MAUREEN.   *(Laughing.)* It's a crazy oul mood you're in for yourself tonight! *(Pause.)* Pleased that tonight it is Pato's leaving and won't be coming pawing me again is what it is, I bet.

MAG.   Maybe that's what it is. I *am* glad Pato's leaving.

MAUREEN.   *(Smiling.)* An interfering oul biddy is all you are. *(Pause.)* Do you want a shortbread finger?

MAG.   I *do* want a shortbread finger.

MAUREEN.   Please.

MAG.   Please. *(Maureen gives Mag a shortbread finger, after waving it phallically in the air a moment.)*

MAUREEN.   Remind me of something, shortbread fingers do.

41

MAG. I suppose they do, now.

MAUREEN. I suppose it's so long since you've seen what they remind me of, you do forget what they look like.

MAG. I suppose I do. And I suppose you're the expert.

MAUREEN. I am the expert.

MAG. Oh aye.

MAUREEN. I'm the king of the experts.

MAG. I suppose you are, now. Oh, I'm sure. I suppose you're the king of the experts.

MAUREEN. *(Pause. Suspicious.)* Why wouldn't you be sure?

MAG. With your Pato Dooley and your throwing it all in me face like an oul peahen, eh? When.... *(Mag catches herself before revealing any more.)*

MAUREEN. *(Pause. Smiling.)* When what?

MAG. Not another word on the subject am I saying. I do have no comment, as they say. This is a nice shortbread finger.

MAUREEN. *(With an edge.)* When what, now?

MAG. *(Getting scared.)* When nothing, Maureen.

MAUREEN. *(Forcefully.)* No, when what, now? *(Pause.)* Have you been speaking to somebody?

MAG. Who would I be speaking to, Maureen?

MAUREEN. *(Trying to work it out.)* You've been speaking to somebody. You've....

MAG. Nobody have I been speaking to, Maureen. You know well I don't be speaking to anybody. And, sure, who would Pato be telling about that...? *(Mag suddenly realises what she's said. Maureen stares at her in dumb shock and hate, then walks to the kitchen, dazed, puts a chip-pan on the stove, turns it on high and pours a half-bottle of cooking oil into it, takes down the rubber gloves that are hanging on the back wall and puts them on. Mag puts her hands on the arms of the rocking-chair to drag herself up, but Maureen shoves a foot against her stomach and groin, ushering her back. Mag leans back into the chair, frightened, staring at Maureen, who sits at the table, waiting for the oil to boil. She speaks quietly, staring straight ahead.)*

MAUREEN. How do you know?

MAG. Nothing do I know, Maureen.

MAUREEN. Uh-huh?

42

MAG. *(Pause.)* Or was it Ray did mention something? Aye, I think it was Ray....

MAUREEN. Nothing to Ray would Pato've said about that subject.

MAG. *(Tearfully.)* Just to stop you bragging like an oul peahen, was I saying, Maureen. Sure what does an oul woman like me know? Just guessing, I was.

MAUREEN. You know sure enough, and guessing me arse, and not on me face was it written. For the second time and for the last time I'll be asking, now. How do you know?

MAG. On your face it *was* written, Maureen. Sure that's the only way I knew. You still do have the look of a virgin about you you always have had. *(Without malice.)* You always will. *(Pause. The oil has started boiling. Maureen rises, turns the radio up, stares at Mag as she passes her, takes the pan off the boil and turns the gas off, and returns to Mag with it. Terrified.)* A letter he did send you I read! *(Maureen slowly and deliberately takes her mother's shrivelled hand, holds it down on the burning range, and starts slowly pouring some of the hot oil over it, as Mag screams in pain and terror.)*

MAUREEN. Where is the letter?

MAG. *(Through screams.)* I did burn it! I'm sorry, Maureen!

MAUREEN. What did the letter say? *(Mag is screaming so much that she can't answer. Maureen stops pouring the oil and releases the hand, which Mag clutches to herself, doubled-up, still screaming, crying and whimpering.)* What did the letter say?

MAG. Said he did have too much to drink, it did! Is why, and not your fault at all.

MAUREEN. And what else did it say?

MAG. He won't be putting me into no home!

MAUREEN. What are you talking about, no home? What else did it say?!

MAG. I can't remember, now, Maureen, I *can't...!* *(Maureen grabs Mag's hand, holds it down again and repeats the torture.)* No...!

MAUREEN. What else did it say?! Eh?!

MAG. *(Through screams.)* Asked you to go to America with him, it did! *(Stunned, Maureen releases Mag's hand and stops pouring the oil. Mag clutches her hand to herself again, whimpering.)*

MAUREEN.   What?

MAG.   But how could you go with him? You do still have me to look after.

MAUREEN.   *(In a happy daze.)* He asked me to go to America with him? Pato asked me to go to America with him?

MAG.   *(Looking up at her.)* But what about me, Maureen? *(A slight pause before Maureen, in a single and almost lazy motion, throws the considerable remainder of the oil into Mag's midriff, some of it splashing up into her face. Mag doubles-up, screaming, falls to the floor, trying to pat the oil off her, and lies there convulsing, screaming and whimpering. Maureen steps out of her way to avoid her fall, still in a daze, barely noticing her.)*

MAUREEN.   *(Dreamily, to herself.)* He asked me to go to America with him...? *(Recovering herself.)* What time is it? Oh feck, he'll be leaving! I've got to see him. Oh God.... What will I wear? Uh.... Me black dress! Me little black dress! It'll be a remembrance to him.... *(Maureen darts off through the hall.)*

MAG.   *(Quietly, sobbing.)* Maureen ... help me.... *(Maureen returns a moment later, pulling her black dress on.)*

MAUREEN.   *(To herself.)* How do I look? Ah, I'll have to do. What time is it? Oh God....

MAG.   Help me, Maureen....

MAUREEN.   *(Brushing her hair.)* Help you, is it? After what you've done? Help you, she says. No, I won't help you, and I'll tell you another thing. If you've made me miss Pato before he goes, then you'll *really* be for it, so you will, and no messing this time. Out of me fecking way, now.... *(Maureen steps over Mag, who is still shaking on the floor, and exits through the front door. Pause. Mag is still crawling around slightly. The front door bangs open and Mag looks up at Maureen as she breezes back in.)* Me car keys I forgot.... *(Maureen grabs her keys from the table, goes to the door, turns back to the table and switches the radio off.)* Electricity. *(Maureen exits again, slamming the door. Pause. Sound of her car starting and pulling off. Pause.)*

MAG.   *(Quietly.)* But who'll look after me, so? *(Mag, still shaking, looks down at her scalded hand. Blackout.)*

Scene 4

Same night. The only light in the room emanates from the orange coals through the grill of the range, just illuminating the dark shapes of Mag, sitting in her rocking-chair, which rocks back and forth of its own volition, her body unmoving, and Maureen, still in her black dress, who idles very slowly around the room, poker in hand.

MAUREEN. To Boston. To Boston I'll be going. Isn't that where them two were from, the Kennedys, or was that somewhere else, now? Robert Kennedy I did prefer over Jack Kennedy. He seemed to be nicer to women. Although I haven't read up on it. *(Pause.)* Boston. It does have a nice ring to it. Better than England it'll be, I'm sure. Although where wouldn't be better than England? No shite I'll be cleaning there, anyways, and no names called, and Pato'll be there to have a say-so anyways if there was to be names called, but I'm sure there won't be. The Yanks do love the Irish. *(Pause.)* Almost begged me, Pato did. Almost on his hands and knees, he was, near enough crying. At the station I caught him, not five minutes to spare, thanks to you. Thanks to your oul interfering. But too late to be interfering you are now. Oh aye. Be far too late, although you did give it a good go, I'll say that for you. Another five minutes and you'd have had it. Poor you. Poor selfish oul bitch, oul you. *(Pause.)* Kissed the face off me, he did, when he saw me there. Them blue eyes of his. Them muscles. Them arms wrapping me. 'Why did you not answer me letter?' And all for coming over and giving you a good kick he was when I told him, but 'Ah no,' I said, 'isn't she just a feeble-minded oul feck, not worth dirtying your boots on?' I was defending you there. *(Pause.)* 'You will come to Boston with me so, me love, when you get up the money.' 'I will, Pato. Be it married or be it living in sin, what do I care? What do I care if tongues'd be wagging? Tongues have wagged about me before, let them wag again. Let them never stop wagging, so long as I'm with you, Pato, what do I care about tongues? So long as it's you and me, and the warmth of us cuddled up, and the skins of us asleep, is all I ever really wanted anyway.' *(Pause.)* 'Except we do still have a problem, what to do with your oul mam, there,' he said. 'Would an oul folks home be too harsh?' 'It wouldn't be too harsh but it would be too expensive.' 'What about your sisters so?' 'Me sisters wouldn't have the bitch. Not even a half-day at Christmas to be with her can them two stand. They clear forgot her birthday this year as well as that. 'How do you stick her without going off your rocker?' they do say to me. Behind her back, like. *(Pause.)* 'I'll leave it up to yourself so,' Pato says. He was on the train be this time, we was kissing out the window, like they do in films. 'I'll leave it up to yourself so, whatever you decide. If it takes a month, let it take a month. And if it's finally you decide you can't bear to be parted from her and have to stay behind, well, I can't say I would like it, but I'd understand. But if even a year it has to take for you to decide, it is a year I will be waiting, and won't be minding the wait.' 'It won't be a year it is you'll be waiting, Pato', I called out then, the train was pulling away. 'It won't be a year nor yet nearly a year. It won't be a week!' *(The rocking-chair has stopped its motions. Mag starts to slowly lean forward at the waist until she finally topples over and falls heavily to the floor, dead. A red chunk of skull hangs from a string of skin at the side of her head. Maureen looks down at her, somewhat bored, taps her on the side with the toe of her shoe, then steps onto her back and stands there in thoughtful contemplation.)* 'Twas over the stile she did trip. Aye. And down the hill she did fall. Aye. *(Pause.)* Aye. *(Pause. Blackout.)*

Scene 5

A rainy afternoon. Front door opens and Maureen enters in funeral attire, takes her jacket off and idles around quietly, her mind elsewhere. She lights a fire in the range, turns the radio on low and sits down in the rocking-chair. After a moment she half-laughs, takes down the boxes of Complan and porridge from the kitchen shelf, goes back to the range and empties the contents of both on the fire. She exits into the hall and returns a moment later with an old suitcase which she lays on the table, brushing off a thick layer of dust. She opens it, considers for a second what she needs to pack, then returns to the hall. There is a knock at the door. Maureen returns, thinks a moment, takes the suitcase off the table and places it to one side, fixes her hair a little, then answers the door.

MAUREEN.   Oh hello there, Ray.

RAY.   *(Off.)* Hello there, Mrs....

MAUREEN.   Come in ahead for yourself.

RAY.   I did see you coming ahead up the road. *(Ray enters, closing the door. Maureen idles to the kitchen and makes herself some tea.)* I didn't think so early you would be back. Did you not want to go on to the reception or the whatyoucall they're having at Rory's so?

MAUREEN.   No. I do have better things to do with me time.

RAY.   Aye, aye. Have your sisters gone on to it?

MAUREEN.   They have, aye.

RAY.   Of course. Coming back here after, will they be?

MAUREEN.   Going straight home, I think they said they'd be.

RAY.   Oh aye. Sure, it's a long oul drive for them. Or fairly long. *(Pause.)* It did all go off okay, then?

MAUREEN.   It did.

RAY.   Despite the rain.

MAUREEN.   Despite the rain.

47

RAY. A poor oul day for a funeral.

MAUREEN. It was. When it could've been last month we buried her, and she could've got the last of the sun, if it wasn't for the hundred bastarding inquests, proved nothing.

RAY. You'll be glad that's all over and done with now, anyways.

MAUREEN. Very glad.

RAY. I suppose they do only have their jobs to do. *(Pause.)* Although no fan am I of the bastarding polis. Me too wee toes they went and broke on me for no reason, me arsehole drunk and disorderly.

MAUREEN. The polis broke your toes, did they?

RAY. They did.

MAUREEN. Oh. Tom Hanlon said what it was you kicked a door in just your socks.

RAY. Did he now? And I suppose you believe a policeman's word over mine. Oh aye. Isn't that how the Birmingham Six went down?

MAUREEN. Sure, you can't equate your toes with the Birmingham Six, now, Ray.

RAY. It's the selfsame differ. *(Pause.)* What was I saying, now?

MAUREEN. Some bull.

RAY. Some bull, is it? No. Asking about your mam's funeral, I was.

MAUREEN. That's what I'm saying.

RAY. *(Pause.)* Was there a big turn-out at it?

MAUREEN. Me sisters and one of their husbands and nobody else but Maryjohnny Rafferty and oul Father Walsh — Welsh — saying the thing.

RAY. Father Welsh punched Mairtin Hanlon in the head once, and for no reason. *(Pause.)* Are you not watching telly for yourself, no?

MAUREEN. I'm not. It's only Australian oul shite they do ever show on that thing.

RAY. *(Slightly bemused.)* Sure, that's why I do like it. Who wants to see Ireland on telly?

MAUREEN. *I* do.

RAY. All you have to do is look out your window to see Ireland. And it's soon bored you'd be. 'There goes a calf.' *(Pause.)* I be bored anyway. I be continually bored. *(Pause.)* London I'm thinking of going to. Aye. Thinking of it, anyways. To work, y'know. One of these days. Or else Manchester. They have a lot more drugs in Manchester. Supposedly, anyways.

MAUREEN. Don't be getting messed up in drugs, now, Ray, for yourself. Drugs are terrible dangerous.

RAY. Terrible dangerous, are they? Drugs, now?

MAUREEN. You know full well they are.

RAY. Maybe they are, maybe they are. But there are plenty of other things just as dangerous, would kill you just as easy. Maybe even easier.

MAUREEN. *(Wary.)* Things like what, now?

RAY. *(Pause. Shrugging.)* This bastarding town for one.

MAUREEN. *(Pause. Sadly.)* Is true enough.

RAY. Just that it takes seventy years. Well, it won't take me seventy years. I'll tell you that. No way, boy. *(Pause.)* How old was your mother, now, when she passed?

MAUREEN. Seventy, aye. Bang on.

RAY. She had a good innings, anyway. *(Pause.)* Or an innings, anyway. *(Sniffs the air.)* What's this you've been burning?

MAUREEN. Porridge and Complan I've been burning.

RAY. For why?

MAUREEN. Because I don't eat porridge or Complan. The remainders of me mother's, they were. I was having a good clear-out.

RAY. Only a waste that was.

MAUREEN. Do I need your say-so so?

RAY. I'd've been glad to take them off your hands, I'm saying.

MAUREEN. *(Quietly.)* I don't need your say-so.

RAY. The porridge, anyway. I do like a bit of porridge. I'd've left the Complan. I don't drink Complan. Never had no call to.

MAUREEN. There's some Kimberleys left in the packet I was about to burn too, you can have, if it's such a big thing.

RAY. I *will* have them Kimberleys. I do love Kimberleys.

MAUREEN. I bet you do. *(Ray eats a couple of Kimberleys.)*

RAY. Are they a bit stale, now? *(Chews.)* It does be hard to tell with Kimberleys. *(Pause.)* I think Kimberleys are me favourite biscuits out of any biscuits. Them or Jaffa Cakes. *(Pause.)* Or Wagon

Wheels. *(Pause.)* Or would you classify Wagon Wheels as biscuits at all now. Aren't they more of a kind of a bar...?

MAUREEN. *(Interrupting.)* I've things to do now, Ray. Was it some reason you had to come over or was it just to discuss Wagon Wheels?

RAY. Oh aye, now. No, I did have a letter from Pato the other day and he did ask me to come up. *(Maureen sits in the rocking-chair and listens with keen interest.)*

MAUREEN. He did? What did he have to say?

RAY. He said sorry to hear about your mother and all, and his condolences he sent.

MAUREEN. Aye, aye, aye, and anything else, now?

RAY. That was the main gist of it, the message he said to pass onto you.

MAUREEN. It had no times or details, now?

RAY. Times or details? No....

MAUREEN. I suppose....

RAY. Eh?

MAUREEN. Eh?

RAY. Eh? Oh, also he said he was sorry he didn't get to see you the night he left, there, he would've liked to've said good-bye. But if that was the way you wanted it, so be it. Although rude, too, I thought that was.

MAUREEN. *(Standing, confused.)* I did see him the night he left. At the station there.

RAY. What station? Be taxicab Pato left. What are you thinking of?

MAUREEN. *(Sitting.)* I don't know now.

RAY. Be taxicab Pato left, and sad that he never got your good-bye, although why he wanted your good-bye I don't know. *(Pause.)* I'll tell you this, Maureen, not being harsh, but your house does smell an awful lot nicer now that your mother's dead. I'll say it does, now.

MAUREEN. Well, isn't that the best? With me thinking I did see him the night he left, there. The train that pulled away. *(He looks at her as if she's mad.)*

RAY. Aye, aye. *(Mumbled, sarcastic.)* Have a rest for yourself. *(Pause.)* Oh, do you know a lass called, em ... Dolores Hooley, or Healey, now? She was over with the Yanks when they was over.

MAUREEN.   I know the name, aye.

RAY.   She was at me uncle's do they had there, dancing with me brother early on. You remember?

MAUREEN.   Dancing with him, was it? Throwing herself at him would be nearer the mark. Like a cheap oul whore.

RAY.   I don't know about that, now.

MAUREEN.   Like a cheap oul whore. And where did it get her?

RAY.   She did seem nice enough to me, there, now. Big brown eyes she had. And I do like brown eyes, me, I do. Oh aye. Like the lass used to be on *Bosco*. Or I *think* the lass used to be on *Bosco* had brown eyes. We had a black and white telly at that time. *(Pause.)* What was I talking about, now?

MAUREEN.   Something about this Dolores Hooley or whoever she fecking is.

RAY.   Oh aye. Herself and Pato did get engaged a week ago, now, he wrote and told me.

MAUREEN.   *(Shocked.)* Engaged to do what?

RAY.   Engaged to get married. What do you usually get engaged for? 'Engaged to do what?' Engaged to eat a bun! *(Maureen is dumbstruck.)* A bit young for him, I think, but good luck to him. A whirlwind oul whatyoucall. July next year, they're thinking of having it, but I'll have to write and tell him to move it either forward or back, else it'll coincide with the European Championships. I wonder if they'll have the European Championships on telly over there at all? Probably not, now, the Yankee bastards. They don't care about football at all. Ah well. *(Pause.)* It won't be much of a change for her anyways, from Hooley to Dooley. Only one letter. The 'h'. That'll be a good thing. *(Pause.)* Unless it's Healey that she is. I can't remember. *(Pause.)* If it's Healey, it'll be three letters. The 'h', the 'e' and the 'a'. *(Pause.)* Would you want me to be passing any message on, now, when I'm writing, Mrs.? I'm writing tomorrow.

MAUREEN.   I get ... I do get confused. Dolores Hooley...?

RAY.   *(Pause. Irritated.)* Would you want me to be passing on any message, now, I'm saying?

MAUREEN.   *(Pause.)* Dolores Hooley...?

RAY.   *(Sighing.)* Fecking.... The loons you do get in this house! Only repeating!

MAUREEN.   Who's a loon?

51

RAY. Who's a loon, she says! *(Ray scoffs and turns away, looking out the window. Maureen quietly picks up the poker from beside the range and, holding it low at her side, slowly approaches him from behind.)*

MAUREEN. *(Angrily.)* Who's a loon?! *(Ray suddenly sees something hidden behind a couple of boxes on the inner window ledge.)*

RAY. *(Angrily.)* Well, isn't that fecking just the fecking best yet...! *(Ray picks up a faded tennis ball with a string sticking out of it from the ledge and spins around to confront Maureen with it, so angry that he doesn't even notice the poker. Maureen stops in her tracks.)* Sitting on that fecking shelf all these fecking years you've had it, and what good did it do ya?! A tenner that swingball set did cost me poor ma and da and in 1979 that was, when a tenner was a lot of money. The best fecking present I did ever get and only two oul months' play out of it I got before you went and confiscated it on me. What right did you have? What right at all? No right. And just left it sitting there then to fade to fecking skitter. I wouldn't't've minded if you'd got some use out of it, if you'd taken the string out and played pat-ball or something agin a wall, but no. Just out of pure spite is the only reason you kept it, and right under me fecking nose. And then you go wondering who's a fecking loon? Who's a fecking loon, she says. I'll tell you who's a fecking loon, lady. *You're* a fecking loon! *(Maureen lets the poker fall to the floor with a clatter and sits in the rocking-chair, dazed.)*

MAUREEN. I don't know why I did keep your swingball on you, Raymond. I can't remember at all, now. I think me head was in a funny oul way in them days.

RAY. 'In them days,' she says, as she pegs a good poker on the floor and talks about trains. *(Ray picks the poker up and puts it in its place.)* That's a good poker, that is. Don't be banging it against anything hard like that, now.

MAUREEN. I won't.

RAY. That's an awful good poker. *(Pause.)* To show there's no hard feelings over me swingball, will you sell me that poker, Mrs.? A fiver I'll give you.

MAUREEN. Ah, I don't want to be selling me poker now, Ray.

RAY. G'wan. Six!

MAUREEN. No. It does have sentimental value to me.

RAY. I don't forgive you, so!

MAUREEN.   Ah, don't be like that, now, Ray....

RAY.   No, I don't forgive you at all.... *(Ray goes to the front door and opens it.)*

MAUREEN.   Ray! Are you writing to your brother, so?

RAY.   *(Sighing.)* I am. Why?

MAUREEN.   Will you be passing a message on from me?

RAY.   *(Sighs.)* Messages, messages, messages, messages! What's the message, so? And make it a short one.

MAUREEN.   Just say.... *(Maureen thinks about it a while.)*

RAY.   This week, if you can!

MAUREEN.   Just say.... Just say, 'The beauty queen of Leenane says hello.' That's all.

RAY.   'The beauty queen of Leenane says hello.'

MAUREEN.   Aye. No! *(Ray sighs again.)* Good-bye. Good-bye. 'The beauty queen of Leenane says good-bye.'

RAY.   'The beauty queen of Leenane says good-bye.' Whatever the feck that means, I'll pass it on. 'The beauty queen of Leenane says good-bye', although after this fecking swingball business, I don't see why the feck I should. Good-bye to you so, Mrs....

MAUREEN.   Will you turn the radio up a biteen too, before you go, there, Pato, now? *Ray,* I mean ...

RAY.   *(Exasperated.)* Feck.... *(Ray turns the radio up.)* The exact fecking image of your mother you are, sitting there pegging orders and forgetting me name! Good-bye!

MAUREEN.   And pull the door after you....

RAY.   *(Shouting angrily.)* I was going to pull the fecking door after me!! *(Ray slams the door behind him as he exits. Pause. Maureen starts rocking slightly in the chair, listening to the song such as one by The Chieftains* on the radio. The announcer's quiet, soothing voice is then heard.)*

ANNOUNCER.   A lovely tune from The Chieftains there. This next one, now, goes out from Annette and Margo Folan to their mother Maggie, all the way out in the mountains of Leenane, a lovely part of the world there, on the occasion of her seventy-first birthday last month now. Well, we hope you had a happy one, Maggie, and we hope there'll be a good many more of them to come on top of it. I'm sure there will. This one's for

---

*See Special Note on Songs and Recordings on copyright page.

you, now. *("The Spinning Wheel"* by Delia Murphy is played. Maureen gently rocks in the chair until about the middle of the fourth verse, when she quietly gets up, picks up the dusty suitcase, caresses it slightly, moves slowly to the hall door and looks back at the empty rocking-chair a while. It is still rocking gently. Slight pause, then Maureen exits into the hall, closing its door behind her as she goes. We listen to the song on the radio to the end, as the chair gradually stops rocking and the lights, very slowly, fade to black.)*

PROPERTY LIST

Shopping items (MAUREEN)
Porridge (MAUREEN)
Porridge pot (MAUREEN)
Spoon (MAUREEN)
Bowl for porridge (MAUREEN)
Tea kettle with water (MAUREEN)
Tea cup or mug with tea (MAUREEN)
Hand mirror (MAG)
Pen (RAY)
Piece of paper (RAY)
Box of matches (MAG)
Sachet of Complan (MAUREEN)
Mug (MAUREEN)
Pack of Kimberley biscuits (MAUREEN)
Potty of urine (MAG)
Black dress (MAG)
Papers (MAG)
Sealed envelope with letter (MAG)
Fire poker (RAY, MAUREEN)
Reading material (MAUREEN)
Shortbread fingers (MAUREEN)
Chip-pan (MAUREEN)
Bottle of cooking oil (MAUREEN)
Rubber gloves (MAUREEN)
Suitcase (MAUREEN)
Ball with string attached (RAY)

SOUND EFFECTS

Rain
Car starting and pulling away